Date Due

OCT 20 1960	NOV 15 '64	
NOV 1 1960	APR 15 65	
FEB 20 1961	FEB 1 '68	MAY 1 '89
		NOV 18 '89
	MAY 15 66	
JUN 1 1961		MAR 13 '90
NOV 1 1961		APR 6 '90
	APR 15 '68	FEB 25 '91
FEB 10 1962	APR 15 '72	
MAR 20 1962	JUN 1 '68	APR 4 '91
OCT 1 1962	MAY 1 '68	APR 25 '91
NOV 1 '63	DEC 1 '86	APR 23 '92
DEC 15 '63	JUN 1 '70	FEB 18 '93
FEB 1 '64	OCT 1 '70	
APR 1 - '64	DEC '70	
APR 1 - '64	MAY '72	
MAY 15 '64	DEC 15 '72	
OCT 1 '64	FEB 1 '73	
OCT 15 '64	FEB 15 '73	
APR 15 '66	MAR 15 '73	
	PRINTED IN U.S.A.	

WILLIAM SHAKESPEARE

William Shakespeare

BY IVOR BROWN

Illustrated by Robert Hodgson

THOMAS NELSON AND SONS LTD EDINBURGH

THOMAS NELSON AND SONS LTD
Parkside Works Edinburgh 9
36 Park Street London W1
312 Flinders Street Melbourne C1

302–304 Barclays Bank Building
Commissioner and Kruis Streets
Johannesburg

THOMAS NELSON AND SONS (CANADA) LTD
91–93 Wellington Street West   Toronto 1

THOMAS NELSON AND SONS
19 East 47th Street New York 17

SOCIÉTÉ FRANÇAISE D'ÉDITIONS NELSON
97 rue Monge Paris 5

———

Printed in Great Britain by
Thomas Nelson and Sons Ltd, Edinburgh

I

PEOPLE now travel to Stratford-upon-Avon from all over
the world. They come because it was the birthplace
and home of an Englishman whose poetry and plays have been
widely famous and are continually read and acted in many
lands. At Stratford the tourists can, during most of the year,
see William Shakespeare's plays well performed in a special
theatre built beside the river Avon in honour of Shakespeare's
memory. They can also see in the town the house where he
was born, and outside it, in near-by villages, the homes of his
mother and of the woman who became his wife. In the church

where Shakespeare was buried there is also the register recording the christening and the burials of himself and his family. It is sometimes said that we know very little about William Shakespeare : as a matter of fact, we know enough to get a fair picture of the place and of the way in which he grew up.

The town Stratford, to which the visitors now flock, has about fifteen thousand people who live there all the year round. It lies close to the Cotswold hill-country, famous for sheep, and to Evesham, famous for orchards. It is a market-town for Midland farmers as well as a Shakespearian Show Place. In that respect its life has gone quietly and steadily on. When Will Shakespeare was born in 1564 Stratford was much smaller than it is now, having probably about two thousand inhabitants. The whole population of Britain was very much less, numbering perhaps five million in the entire country instead of our fifty million. London, with its suburbs, was then about the size of Aberdeen or Dundee in the Scotland of today, or of Southampton in England.

Many of the old towns were built at fords or bridges over rivers. At Cambridge the river Cam was bridged and at Oxford the oxen could, except in time of flood, be safely driven through a shallow part of the Thames. So these towns were renowned as places for the traveller and the farmer long before they acquired their Colleges and became frequented by teachers and students. Stratford grew from a riverside village to be quite important because it was a link between the east and west of central England. Though the word Stratford now suggests Shakespeare to us, it was known long before and long after his time for its crossing of the river Avon.

Its name is really Street-ford. Then, to the ford was added a fine bridge with fourteen arches. It is still there and used to this day. Its building was arranged by a rich Stratford man called Hugh Clopton : his life, which ended seventy-two years before Shakespeare was born, was rather like Dick Whittington's, since he went to the capital in search of his fortune and became Lord Mayor of London. He is remembered now by the long, handsome, but narrow bridge on which the heavy traffic of to-day comes crowding in. But it is the same bridge that Shakespeare used when he travelled to and from London, while he was winning fame rather than a fortune. As an actor and poet he could not in those days become Lord Mayor of the capital, but it is just as well for posterity that he stuck to his art and sold his writing instead of merchandise.

It is wrong to think of Stratford then as a mere village whose people were mostly ignorant peasants. It was a busy town with a good Grammar School, its own Town Council, and a fine church. The merchants of country produce and the craftsmen who made clothes and saddlery and furnishings, were usually prosperous. They saved money, bought land, and were apt to quarrel over their property and unpaid debts. The local lawyers found good employment in conducting their

disputes. There were famous castles and mansions round about, notably at Warwick and Kenilworth, where Queen Elizabeth herself was a visitor. The great lords liked to have plays and pageants, and collected teams of actors, some of whom performed in Stratford itself. It was indeed a lively place for a clever boy. He could have good teaching, he could greet the exciting arrival of the players, and he had all the country sports of fishing, hunting and hawking to watch or to share.

William Shakespeare's father was a maker and seller of gloves and other leather goods, and he may have also dealt

4

in the beasts whose skins he used for his work. He was an important person in the town and at one time was its Chamberlain, which meant that he kept the borough accounts. He had married Mary Arden, a member of a well-known and fairly rich Midland family, and he had two neighbouring houses in Henley Street, one of which is now called 'The Birthplace' and is much visited. Mary Arden's childhood home at Wilmcote, three miles away, is also worth visiting; it shows what a well-equipped farm house was like in those days, and still contains the tools and gear and furniture of the time.

William Shakespeare was christened in the Parish Church

of Stratford on 25 April 1564. As christenings were then carried out as soon as possible after birth, it has been assumed that he was born on 23 April, and that day is kept as The Birthday every year. Flags of all the nations are displayed, people go in a procession to the Church, carrying flowers to put on the tomb, and there is a lot of speech-making. And, of course, there is play-acting too. Nothing would more surprise the people who lived in Stratford in Shakespeare's boyhood than to find out that young Will had made their town so famous and so much visited from afar. I have written of him as Will, rather than with the full and formal name of William, for that is how his friends spoke and wrote of him and how, also, he wrote of himself in some of his poems.

Stratford, as has been explained, was by no means a poor little place as towns went then. But even the richest persons and places suffered from severe dangers and disadvantages, if their way of life be compared with our own. For example, the doctors had very crude notions of how to cope with illness —and there was a great deal of illness. This was partly because the people had nothing like our system of drains and regulated water-supply, and partly because their food was limited to what they could produce for themselves.

So there were no imported fruits or vegetables. Children then did not get orange-juice or a carefully balanced diet. And there were no tests of the milk and no treatment of it to prevent infection. During the winter they had, like their

6

parents, to go on eating meat which had been killed at the end of the summer and then had been salted for keeping. When the autumn fruits, apples and pears and plums, were finished, the people had monotonous, unhealthy meals with too much salt meat. They also relied much on pigeons for extra dishes and each farm had a big dove-cote to house the birds : at Wilmcote you can see a fine example of this. But one does not want pigeon-pie every day. Our world, with its ' deep-freeze ' and canning of fruits and vegetables, gives us a much better change of dishes and a much better chance of keeping healthy in winter. Furthermore, we are careful to see that supplies of milk and water are kept as pure as possible.

The towns, big and small, were frequently ravaged by plague. What sort of plague this was, we do not know for certain. There may have been several kinds of epidemic. What is certain is their severity and their power to kill. In the year of Will Shakespeare's birth, plague raged in Stratford and whole families were wiped out. At least two hundred and fifty cases were fatal ; that is to say, one-eighth of the population was destroyed. (Incidentally, fire was another great peril to the houses, and there again Stratford, with no skilled fire-brigade, suffered great loss from time to time.) It was the custom for those who could to leave a plague-visited town. It is a fair guess that Will's mother took her new-born son away to the farm at Wilmcote or elsewhere in the country during that terrible summer and autumn.

His life would be the more precious to his parents since they had already lost two children in infancy, both girls, from one misfortune or another. Nowadays we think the loss of a baby to be a rare and terrible affliction in a good home, but the Elizabethans were accustomed to these disasters. John and Mary Shakespeare had eight children in all, three of whom, all girls, died in early childhood. Will's three brothers died at the ages of forty-six, thirty-nine and twenty-seven. He himself died at fifty-two, which we call middle-age ; when he was thirty-two he had lost his only son, who was then a boy of eleven. Both his parents and their one surviving daughter had long lives, but, on the whole, the Shakespeares were not, by our standards, a healthy family. People did not then expect to live nearly as long as we do now. Illness, when it came, was hard to combat. There were no inoculations and nothing like the range of medicines and disinfectants that we possess.

Children were then very strictly brought up ; both at home and at school they were taught to obey, and were subject to rules and punishments which we would now think extremely severe. Young Will Shakespeare, if the general practice was followed in his case, would be sent to the Grammar School of Stratford at the age of seven. It cannot be proved that he did go there, because the School Register has been lost. But where else would he have gone ? There would be a ' free place ' for him, as the son of a Town Councillor, until he was sixteen. The School was of sound repute and the high salary of its Head

Master attracted a series of scholars from Oxford University to look after it. Visitors can still see the timbered frontage of the old building beside the grey Chapel of the Guild, but, of course, it is much larger now and has new buildings behind the old.

Lessons in the schools of that time began at six o'clock in summer and seven in winter and went on until five, with a play-interval of fifteen minutes at three. There were breaks for breakfast at nine and for dinner at eleven. That was a very long day, and Saturday was not a whole holiday, only a half-day. The boys, having been up so early, must have had quite enough of it when five o' clock came. Shakespeare wrote later in life of

> . . . *the whining schoolboy with his satchel*
> *And shining morning face, creeping like snail*
> *Unwillingly to school*

and also of how, after the school breaks up,

> *Each hurries to his home and sporting-place.*

No doubt he often resented having to rise so early and scrub his cheeks till they shone. He would be ready for that quick escape at five. But it is happily suggested that he and his friends still had energy for play.

The earliest schooling was done with a Horn Book or Absey Book (A.B.C. Book). This was a spelling sheet mounted on wood with a transparent horn cover, and therefore difficult to lose or damage. Singing was carefully taught. The Bible, in an earlier translation than the one we have, was read. Latin lessons began early and were the basis of all subsequent schooling. The chief text-book was Lily's Grammar, and that is mentioned and quoted in Shakespeare's plays, As they advanced, the boys went on to the Latin classics, and Shakespeare always remembered the fables and romances in the poetry of Ovid.

If the Stratford Grammar School was like others of the same period, about which we have more details, there was no mercy for the idle or the mischievous. It was believed by parents and teachers that the rod was God's instrument for driving the devil out of children, and the 'jerks', as they were called, of the cane or birch were frequently administered. Whether Shakespeare enjoyed his early years it is hard to say. Late in life he was to write, with obvious feeling, of the happy innocence of boyhood when two lads regarded it bliss to be 'boy eternal' while they frisked like lambs in the sun. But that may be the sentimental reflection of one who long ago was freed from the snail-creep to lessons, from the long hours, and from the 'jerks'.

Three school-masters appear as characters in his plays, and all are made ridiculous. He was a man of the widest sympathies, but he never put to paper any compassionate tribute to the teacher who had also to go through long hours, striving to keep the troublesome or drowsy class awake on hot afternoons, and to drum some knowledge into reluctant heads. During his time

at the Grammar School one of the headmasters was a Welshman, Thomas Jenkins. There is a portrait of a Welsh schoolmaster, Sir Hugh Evans, in Shakespeare's comedy, *The Merry Wives of Windsor*, and that may be a memory of Jenkins. Evans is no harsh tyrant and is easily persuaded to give the boys an extra holiday, but he is presented as a ludicrous fellow and laughed at for making, in his Welsh way, 'fritters' of the English language.

Unless Will Shakespeare was what we call 'a late developer' he must have been a very quick learner, and he obviously enjoyed his Latin when he got away from grammar to poetry, and could read tales of events that haunted his memory throughout his life. He wrote in contempt of 'continual plodders' who win little, and he mocked the pedantical kind of usher in the person of Holofernes in *Love's Labour's Lost*, who was for ever spouting Latin and showing off his silly kind of scholarship. We may therefore guess that he never had a teacher with imagination who could stimulate the fancy of a potentially brilliant boy. Those headmasters from Oxford were sound men, no doubt, but they probably kept to their routine and lacked sympathy for an unusual pupil who may have been wayward and scornful of the dull drudgery of the ordinary lessons.

Discipline was usually strict in the home, and the children

had to wait on their parents at table as well as help with the washing-up. But there is no reason to suppose that John and Mary Shakespeare were unduly severe, and there is a pleasing reference in one play to fond fathers who bind up

> *. . . the threatening twigs of birch*
> *Only to stick it in their children's sight*
> *For terror, not to use*

so that the rod became ' more mock'd than feared '. There may well be a memory of domestic clemency in this, either in the behaviour of his own father or in his own position as a parent later on.

A certain mystery hangs over the affairs of the Shakespeare family while Will was reaching the age for leaving school. His father was in some kind of trouble, perhaps because he disagreed with the religious doctrines prevailing in the town, perhaps because his business affairs were not going as well as they had done. Whatever the cause, he seems to have dropped out of the public life of Stratford in which he had once been so active.

His last son, Edmund, who later in life followed Will to London and became an actor in the theatre of the capital, was born in 1580. John Shakespeare had then five children on his hands and, if he had less money coming in, he had also more to pay out. He could not afford, or did not choose, to send William to Oxford, which was the obvious next step for a boy who had shown capacity at school. (Oxford, being only forty miles away, was a likelier University for Stratford boys than was Cambridge, which lay at the end of a long cross-country journey.) The pace of life was much quicker then than it is now, and boys went to the University at fourteen or even less, leaving at sixteen or seventeen, when they were judged to be grown men. So, if Will had been sent to an Oxford college, he would have gone there about 1578. We do not know when he left school, but it was probably about that time. No doubt he was precocious and eager to get on with his life and to be an asset, not a burden, to his family. Later he wrote, 'The spirit of a youth, that means to be of note, begins betimes.'

Unfortunately we have no certain knowledge about his next step. One of the early suggestions was made by John Aubrey, a gossiping compiler of notes about the lives of famous men. He did not write until a hundred years after Shakespeare's boyhood, but he did get his information from an actor whose father had been a member of Shakespeare's company. Aubrey stated that Will was 'in his younger years a schoolmaster in the country.' That is likely enough, but, not having a University degree, he would have had to occupy a humble post, beginning as pupil-teacher or minor usher. We can be sure that he would have been a most unusual teacher, amusing, enlivening and most encouraging to any child of promise. On the other hand, the mockery of schoolmasters in his plays and his lack of sympathy with their troubles in coping with slow or obstreperous pupils, may be a reason for doubting whether he ever did take up teaching.

It is possible that Aubrey was partly correct when he wrote of the young Shakespeare's early days in the teaching profession. The boy may well have gone, not to a school, but as assistant in some great nobleman's house. These rich men then often employed 'pages', a term which covered all sorts of duties, not just answering the bell, but doing secretarial work or acting as tutor to the children of the family. Michael Drayton, another poet of this period, served as 'a proper, goodly page' in the mansion of Sir Harry Goodere at Polesworth in the same county

as Stratford, and Drayton has described how happily he read the classics and learned to be a writer while thus established in the household. If Will had gone as a page of this kind into one of the big houses, he could have had the freedom of a library and learned the ways of fine living, all useful preparation for the work he was to do as a writer of poems and plays based on old classical legends, on histories, and on the adventures of wealthy and elegant men and women.

In these great families music-making was general and the page would be expected to take his part in that. It is obvious from Shakespeare's own writing that he was devoted to music, and the boys who joined theatrical companies were expected

to be musicians. If this idea of the young Shakespeare as 'page' is correct, he may have been taken into one of the great Gloucestershire families, such as that of the Earl of Berkeley, for he seems to have known the near-by Cotswold country well and to have had some special knowledge of Berkeley Castle.

Another guess is that William was put into a lawyer's office. In that way of life there would be plenty of scope ; there was much legal business, as I have explained, in this country town where the farmers were so ready to bicker over pieces of land or debts that were owed. The idea of a lawyer's career has been put forward because in the words used by Shakespeare in his writings there are so many terms and phrases taken from the language of the law. He obviously knew this language well, and with great skill he worked it into his prose and poetry. Hamlet pours out a whole string of legal terms in his talk with the Grave-digger ; yet Hamlet had not been trained as a lawyer.

It is quite likely, of course, that Will tried several jobs, doing one period in a school and another with a lawyer. We can imagine him as being restless and discontented with the life of a country town and dreaming of an escape to London and a larger kind of life. A friend of his called Richard Field, whose father sold leather to John Shakespeare for his glove-making, did go off to London when William was fifteen. Field was 'prenticed to a printing business, married his master's

daughter, and became head of the firm. In 1594 he printed
the first of Will's printed books, when he, too, was becoming
successful in the capital. The departure of young Field may
have made Will more fidgety than ever. In his early plays
there are several references to the desire of ambitious young
men for travel.

> *Some to the wars, to try their fortunes there,*
> *Some to discover islands far away,*
> *Some to the studious Universities.*

It has been suggested that Shakespeare did go to the wars in
Europe before he settled down, and that he did have a taste of
a sailor's life ; but there is no proof of either contention. What
we can guess with some confidence is that he had a great in-
clination ' to see the wonders of the world abroad ' or at least
to have a taste of London, since ' home-keeping youth hath
ever homely wits '. Perhaps the author of these lines was
looking back to a time when he found himself too much at
home to feel contented.

His home-life was added to by an early marriage. He was
only eighteen when he wedded Ann Hathaway whose family
home at Shottery, a mile from Stratford, is well preserved and
much visited. She was a farmer's daughter and seven years
older than her husband. Their ages were strangely unequal,
but it was an enduring marriage. Though Will was to be
away so much, writing and acting in London and journeying

with his fellow-players on tour, he is said to have revisited Stratford once a year, and certainly he came back to settle down and enjoy the peace of the country with his wife at his side after the hard work of his life in the theatre. There were three children of the marriage. First came Susanna, born in 1583, and then twins, Hamnet, a boy, and Judith, a girl, born in 1585.

At some time after the birth of the twins Will left Stratford to join a company of players. The tale was told, but not till more than a hundred years after the possible event, that he had to go because of trouble with the local land-owner and magistrate, Sir Thomas Lucy of Charlecote : the story alleged that Will was one of a tough young company who were caught poaching deer in Sir Thomas's park. It was said that Lucy had him ' oft whipped and sometimes imprisoned ', and at last forced him to leave the district.

But the facts are that Sir Thomas had no deer-park at the time, and the severe penalties mentioned would not have been legal. It is possible, however, that the tale of Lucy's deer was an exaggerated version of a slighter poaching escapade into which Will had ventured with some ' lads of the village '. When a local boy has ' made good ' it is common for the local gossips to invent yarns about his riotous youth : these appeal to readers later on and build up a romance. But they need checking, and checking in this case destroys the legend of a whipped and imprisoned Will Shakespeare. However, this need not deter Stratford visitors from driving four miles out to Charlecote where the Lucys' old home is open to the public, and where there is a handsome herd of deer in the park beside the Avon. Whether or not the young Shakespeare did become a poacher, this is very much Shakespeare's England.

The people of Stratford had ample chance to see and listen to 'strolling players', the

teams of actors who left London from time to time and went round the towns of the countryside. They carried the name and wore the livery of a wealthy lord who was their patron and protector.

They needed protection because actors had only the position of ' vagabonds ' in the eyes of the law, and such folk were considered to be avoiding honest labour when useful labour might be much required. If they had the title and uniform of Lord So-and-So's Men they were left alone, as the patron was deemed responsible for their good service in their own calling. Between the years 1573 and 1587, that is during the most impressionable years of Will's boyhood and youth, there were constant visits of players to Stratford. This we know because they had to get a licence from the Town Council to perform. One of the troupes several times in Stratford had for patron the Earl of Berkeley, whose castle in Gloucestershire has already been mentioned as a possible place of employment for Will as a page.

When the boy was eleven Queen Elizabeth made one of her journeys to stay with a favourite courtier, the Earl of Leicester, at Kenilworth Castle, and there was much gorgeous pageantry provided. It is likely enough that people flocked to the Castle grounds to watch these sumptuous shows, and it is a curious fact that a water-pageant, fully described by an actor and musician called Laneham who was there, seems to be described again in Oberon's speech in Shakespeare's play,

A Midsummer Night's Dream, where there is mention of a spectacle with ' a mermaid on a dolphin's back '. John Shakespeare's family could have ridden over—a matter of eleven miles—to join the entranced and applauding Warwickshire folk on the fringe of these high revels.

So, with play-acting and poetry and music not far away, and often in the town of Stratford itself, Will may well have felt that here was the life for him. How tedious, after such pleasures, would be the class-room or the lawyer's office ! In 1587, five years after Shakespeare's marriage, Lord Leicester's Men were touring in this region and visited Stratford ; they had with them a famous clown or comedian, Will Kemp, who was subsequently a partner of Shakespeare's in London. So some have naturally surmised that this was the occasion when Will volunteered his services, reading something that he had written or showing what he could do as an actor, and that he was then accepted as a recruit to the company. That, of course, is a guess. But it is certain that about this time he did leave Stratford to take his chance in London with the new profession in which he was to win fame and to flourish in reward as in renown.

It can hardly have been a popular choice with his family. There were his wife and three children to clothe and feed ; there were his father and mother, now suffering some lack of their old prosperity. How was the runaway to provide for any of them ? Would he earn enough to send sufficient money home ? And was not this a very risky profession to join ? To the responsible Stratford families it would seem a dreadful choice to make, and one can easily imagine the comments of scandalised neighbours. Oh yes, young Dick Field had gone away to London, but that was to a proper job with a well-known printer. But to be a strolling player was very different. Those players, it would be said, were a shifty, vagabond lot, despite the patronage of Lords, and were never secure. They were in and out of work, and sometimes in and out of prison. While the neighbours sniffed, Will's wife may have sobbed and scolded. Where was she to look for her housekeeping money ? Somehow Will may have pacified her, given what savings he had—he was ever thrifty in money matters—and calmed her with confident promises of great things to come. As he promised, so he performed. The great things did come. The world owes much to the day when Will Shakespeare made his brave decision and left Stratford for a larger world.

2

A YOUNG man whose head was throbbing with ideas and fancies and fine words to express them would nowadays be most inclined to seek a career by working for a newspaper. This, if he could obtain a trial and prove himself capable, would provide him with some regular income ; enough, at least, for his bread and butter. If he was eager to write books or plays he could do so in his spare time : that would be hard work, but it would be an outlet for the ambitions of the energetic. Many famous authors have begun in this way. A notable example was J. M. Barrie, who went to London as a journalist before he took to writing the plays which made him so successful.

For Will Shakespeare there were no such openings, because there was then no regular profession of journalism. But fortunately there was growing up in London a new, busy, and exciting way of life for young men who could use a pen. There were careers to be found in the theatre. The payments made to the authors of the plays were small, but where else could the would-be writers turn ? So into this world of actors came the young men from Oxford and Cambridge who were known as University Wits. Shakespeare had not been to the

University, but he had his wits about him. He was soon to prove that he could be as fluent and as witty as any of the men with a college background in the service of the theatre.

Previously the English drama had been mainly written and performed as a labour of love and of religious devotion. The Miracle Plays, as they were called in the Middle Ages, had been versions of Bible stories, devoutly prepared and acted by workers in the various industries on the Holy Days (holidays also) of the Church. The craftsmen naturally chose subjects to suit their own skill ; the carpenters, for example, would enact the story of the Ark and build a mimic ship for Noah and his family and the animals. These plays were given in the open, outside Churches, after pageants or processions through the streets. The procedure was all very simple and could be amusing as well as instructive. There was then no idea that religious plays had to be only solemn and rather dull. The Feast Days were to be festive.

But the world of the play-makers changed rapidly in the reign of Queen Elizabeth. A new kind of play, which was not religious, had begun to be popular. Naturally the workers in the Craft Guilds, who had given their open-air performances for the glory of God, did not make the members of the public pay for seats ; but now the new kind of drama attracted play-goers who were ready to pay. This meant that the actors and authors could also be paid. What had been a sacred pastime now became a work-a-day profession.

Sometimes the new acting took place in the yards of the inns, which were built with galleries round the central space into which the coaches and carriages were driven. There are very few such inn-yards left now, but one can be seen at Gloucester, and the remnants of one at Southwark in South London. The latter remains close to where Shakespeare lived and worked at the height of his career. It is easy to see that such places would make natural theatres if a platform were raised at the closed-in end of the yard. But regular theatres were also being built in London for the benefit of the rising industry of entertainment.

The first of these had been put up when Shakespeare was a boy of twelve. This was called The Theatre, as though there could be no other. But soon there were others. All theatres had to be outside the City of London because its rulers, grave and serious people, afraid of anything novel, thought that the plays and players were a public nuisance. They said that the

plays pictured crime and vice, and that the crowds who came to see them were a low-down lot and likely to contain idle, disorderly, and thievish persons. So the builder of The Theatre chose Shoreditch, which lay safely to the north of the City boundary. Then another play-house called The Curtain was set beside it : this proved that there were plenty of customers willing to pay for the plays and shows provided.

The success of these houses led to further building on the south of the Thames. There was only one bridge over the river then, Old London Bridge, with its north end in the City and its south end on what was known as the South Bank, outside the City. There were big gates beside it, which were locked at night to keep out bad characters ; so travellers arriving late had to lodge outside till the morning. This meant that there were many inns in Southwark and since that suburb was out-side the City rule, places of entertainment could be set up there and do a good business. A play-house called The Rose was erected and another called The Swan followed it.

Moreover, there was a pleasure-ground called Paris Garden, where there were sports which we would regard as disgustingly cruel. Bulls and bears were baited with dogs, and there was much shedding of blood as the dogs, usually mastiffs, tore at the throats of the animals and were themselves savagely bitten by the bears and tossed by the infuriated bulls. It is odd to think that Shakespeare's exquisite and tender lines, as well as his battle-poetry, were often spoken with the harsh din of these

30

contests and of their cheering spectators as the background music.

If we are right in thinking that Shakespeare came to London in 1587 when he was twenty-three, this was an exciting time for his arrival. There were great fears of a perilous war with Spain, but these fears were mainly banished by the great victory over the Spanish Armada in the following year. (I said 'mainly banished' because all through Shakespeare's early years in London, Spain was still a powerful enemy and various naval raids went on. There was always war in the offing.)

There was also, which concerned him more closely, a great stir in this new profession of writing and acting. One of the University Wits, a man called Christopher Marlowe, who had been schooled at Canterbury and had then gone on to Cambridge, was rousing much admiration and excitement by the vigorous poetry and blood-and-thunder excitements of his play (in two parts) called *Tamburlaine*. It told the story of an Eastern shepherd who became a mighty and merciless conqueror. It showed the horrors of his wars and crimes. It far excelled, in the splendour of its poetry, all the plays that had gone before. It was sumptuously dressed, and a famous player of the day called Edward Alleyn, who later on founded Dulwich College in South London, made a tremendous success in the chief part.

Shakespeare would naturally go to hear Marlowe and to see Alleyn, and their joint hold on the public would make him anxious to take his part at once in this great writing game. There is proof that Shakespeare greatly admired Marlowe, and his early plays showed that he was ready to follow Marlowe fairly closely in the writing of lusty, fine-sounding lines.

To make such verbal music, and make money too—what a life that would be ! We must always think of the Stratford that lay a hundred miles away when we are thinking of Shakespeare's youth in London. He had to find cash to send home ; he had to prove that his decision to join the players was a right one. This proof he was to provide amply within ten years ; meanwhile the start had to be made. Marlowe and Alleyn were examples of how to do it.

Long after Shakespeare's lifetime stories were told about his youth. I have mentioned the anecdote about Sir Thomas Lucy's deer-park. There was another tale that young Will looked after the horses of play-goers who came mounted to the theatre and needed what we might call a ' horse-park '. It was said that Will showed such a good sense of management that he built up quite a rich business in this way. There may be something in it. Perhaps at one time, when he lacked a part to act or a play to work on, he may have run a side-line in horse-watching. But if he were attached to a company of actors when he came to London, its members would have quickly realised that they had acquired a lad of singular capacity, and would not have let him devote much of his time to seeking pocket-money outside his proper work.

A great deal of argument has been carried on concerning the company or companies for which Shakespeare first worked. We need not bother now about these disputed details. What is certain is that within some seven years of leaving Stratford he held an important position with the Lord Chamberlain's Men. This was a very important team which had taken over the plays, properties and privileges of the Queen's Men, the great Queen Elizabeth's own favourite troupe, who had to provide special entertainment for the Court at Christmas and on high State occasions. We have the record that together with Will Kemp, the comedian, and Richard Burbage, a serious actor who was to be the greatest 'star' of his time, Shakespeare was a recipient of considerable sums from the Royal purse for two performances at Greenwich Palace at Christmas, 1594.

With this company, which changed its name to the King's Men when James VI of Scotland, a great patron of plays and players, succeeded Elizabeth as James I of England in 1603, Shakespeare continued throughout the twenty or more years of his working life.   Other writers moved from theatre to theatre, serving several companies.   Shakespeare, after his emergence, worked only for one.   Kemp left the team, but Burbage was another who stayed on faithfully, appearing continually in the chief parts in Shakespeare's plays.   It must have been a friendly, as well as a prosperous, partnership.   Artists of all kinds, and actors not least, are nervous and excitable people and quarrel easily over their work.   No doubt Shakespeare's workmates had their rows, but the team did not break up.

The companies, or Fellowships of Players, as they were sometimes called, were organised under the patronage and protection of royalty and nobility for reasons of safety which I have already explained.   They consisted of three classes of actor.   At the top were the seniors who were called Sharers because they divided the profits with the owner of the theatre, who was called the Housekeeper.   (When a new theatre was built, the Sharers might find the money, do the job themselves, and so be their own Housekeepers.   This happened when Shakespeare and his partners built themselves the Globe Theatre on the South Bank of the Thames in 1599.)   Next to the Sharers came the Hired Men, who played minor roles for a wage and did not share the profits.   Thirdly there were the Boy Players.

These Boy Players were very important because there were no actresses then.   The theatre was thought too rough a place for women to work in, and it was not till 1660—in the reign of

Charles II—that women were allowed on public stages. They could, however, even the most noble of birth, including Queens, take part in Masques at Court. Masques were a mixture of play and dance and performed chiefly by amateurs in a gay and casual manner ; but the words and scenery were carefully prepared by professionals.

It is plain that Shakespeare trusted the powers of the Boy Players, since he wrote such big and testing women's parts which they would have to tackle. It would be foolish to write a play like *Romeo and Juliet* or *As You Like It* if the author was not sure, or at least very hopeful, that those huge roles, containing the sorrows of Juliet in the former and the wit of Rosalind in the latter play, could be successfully ' put across ', as we say, by the young male talent in the company. It is worth noting that Ben Jonson, both a friend and a rival of Shakespeare, wrote a poem on the death of a Boy Player called Pavy, who died at the age of thirteen : in it he said that Pavy had acted so well that Death mistook the child for an old man, and that for three years little Pavy had been ' the stage's jewel '. So the boy had begun, and succeeded, very early.

These children were apprenticed to Sharers for two or three years, and the Sharers had to teach them their business. This would include fencing and music, for there was a great deal of fighting by the characters in the dramas of the time, and the craft of mimic sword-play would have to be mastered

35

early. Music too was most important. There were frequently songs for boys' treble voices, as well as instrumental music in which they could be trained to take a valuable part. The nuisance for the Sharers was that the boys on whom they spent so much trouble grew up so quickly : they soon became too tall and muscular for young women's parts and their voices broke and became masculine. An accident of that kind must have happened during the rehearsal or subsequent performance of a late play of Shakespeare's called *Cymbeline*. In it he wrote a most beautiful song for two boys to sing, the one which begins ' Fear no more the heat of the sun '. But it became necessary to explain that their voices have now got ' the mannish crack ' and therefore they must ' word '—i.e. speak—the lines instead of singing them.

We may guess that the boy apprentices were kept hard at it ; they had to be versatile, vigorous and quick to learn their lines, for new plays with long women's parts in them were constantly being staged. But they were kindly remembered by their old masters. When Augustine Phillips, one of Shakespeare's fellow-actors in the King's Men, died in 1605 he left gifts in money and gold to his senior colleagues. Then for

36

his former pupils, boy players or once boy players, he made a kindly addition :

> Item, I geve to Samuell Gilborne my late apprentice, the some of fortye shillings, and my mouse colloured velvit hose, and a white taffety dublet, a blacke taffety sute, my purple cloke, sword and dagger, and my base viall. Item I geve to James Sands my Apprentice the some of fortye shillings and a citterne a bandore and a lute, to be paid and delivered unto him at the expiration of his terme of yeres in his indenture of apprenticehood.

(Taffety, or taffeta, was a cloth used in fine apparel ; the viall, citterne, bandore and lute were musical instruments.)

There were also companies composed wholly of boys, and their members would have to handle parts of both sexes and of all ages. Young Pavy, who played greybeards so cleverly, was a member of one of these juvenile teams. He belonged to the Children of the Chapel, who provided the Queen's Revels and later on gave public performances at a theatre in

Blackfriars. There are some lines in Shakespeare's play of *Hamlet* which show that the children were so much in fashion and were so much applauded that the senior actors were losing favour and becoming jealous. This rivalry between old and young went on for some time, but there was a change in 1608, quite late in Shakespeare's working life, when his company, the King's Men, took over the Blackfriars Theatre. The Boys still carried on elsewhere, but they had lost some of their popularity and power to attract.

The actors of that time had to be ready to go anywhere and perform on any kind of platform. Learned men have argued much about the shape and size of the regular theatres and their stages in North London and on the South Bank. The details of that complicated argument need not bother us. What must be understood is that a theatre of this kind was only the home or headquarters of the players who were frequently summoned to perform in all sorts of places, perhaps at the Queen's Palace or in a nobleman's mansion or at the halls of the men of law. These calls were much valued, for such performances were better paid in money than were those in ordinary theatres.

When the players went touring they had to act in inn-yards or town-halls or in the halls of big country houses. They could carry very little luggage, just a few wigs and changes of costume. They relied very little upon scenery and careful rehearsal planned to suit a certain shape of stage. That would have been useless if they were always acting in different conditions. In *Hamlet* there is a clear example of what the players could expect when travelling. We see a troupe admitted to the Danish Castle and ordered to act one from the list of plays which they knew. They set to work and mimed and spoke it, without more ado. There was none of the elaborate planning which we call 'production' nowadays.

So the acting which Shakespeare saw and heard when he came to London was probably loud, vigorous and simple. We are used to subtle pictures of characters, but when Alleyn, the first player of his day, spoke the mighty lines of *Tamburlaine* we may be sure that he was audible in sound and terrible in aspect. The writers of plays mainly used prose for comedy and verse for history and tragedy, a habit which Shakespeare followed. The serious actors roared out their lines like those trained in the art of public speaking, while the clowns went their own gay way and put in jokes of their own invention to set the audience roaring with laughter. Shakespeare resented their additions to his own text, just as he resented the excessive noise and grimacing of the serious actors.

The specially built theatres of Shakespeare's London were, as a rule, set round a platform which ran out into the middle of an uncovered yard. The members of the audience who paid least were known as 'the groundlings'. They had no roof over them and stood in the yard, right round the platform. Behind them were tiers of more expensive seats which had

roofs and to which ladies could be brought. Behind the actors'
front platform was a portion of stage with a canopy over it,
and behind that was a recessed room for indoor scenes with a
gallery above it ; this gallery could be used by musicians or
by actors supposed to be standing on a tower, balcony, or city
wall. We do not know whether there were printed programmes,
but if you listen closely to a Shakespeare play, you will notice
that the place is usually mentioned in the words spoken
while characters are introduced with some such phrase as
'Look, where he comes,' after a name has been given.

In these public theatres the performances were given by
daylight in the afternoons and ran from about two to half past

four. But there were indoor theatres, like that at Blackfriars, where the performances were later and lamps and candles were used. Much was written at the time, sometimes by disappointed writers of plays, about the rowdiness and rudeness of the audience : there certainly was much cracking of nuts, munching of apples, and swilling of beer during a play which was dull, but other writers have praised the silent attention of the crowd when the play pleased them. So we can say that the audiences, like the plays, were of all sorts. The cruder patrons could look forward through a serious play to the 'jig' that would follow it. This was a short comedy or farce with song and dance in which the clowns of the company appeared.

In some of Shakespeare's plays the clowns and comic actors have almost nothing to do, and they had to be given a chance to please their 'fans', as we call admirers now. The jig was their outlet. It seems very odd to us that the greatest tragedies were supplemented with these antics.

Most people today, if they are interested at all in plays and performances, see much more acting on the screen than in a theatre. It may be the screen of a picture-house or the screen of a television set at home. In either case the player is acting under powerful lights, close to a powerful camera, and with microphones to record or transmit the sound of his voice. In these conditions the type of acting and speaking that will be effective on a screen is of a small, intimate kind, and this kind of acting has also become admired on the stage today. Shouting and pulling faces are fatal with cameras and 'mikes' around. But the various kinds of stage for which Shakespeare wrote, and on which his players moved and spoke his poetry, needed big, strong, storming methods. Therefore Burbage and the others would probably seem crude to us, who are used to much gentler speaking and more subtle portrayal of character.

Shakespeare himself mocked at the overacting that went on in his time and said that the ears of the audience were split by the raging and ranting of the players. So we must not think how wonderful it would be to be carried back on a magic carpet to see Shakespeare and his company, and to see the first rendering of one of Shakespeare's plays. Such a marvel would be enormously interesting, because we could answer all sorts of questions which historians and students have been asking for centuries. But I very much doubt whether, by our standards, we should admire the acting at all. Probably we would think that a first-rate company, such as we get at Stratford-upon-Avon or the 'Old Vic', in London, would show a more delicate skill as well as making a far more satisfactory picture.

Actors who were often on the move and summoned here and there to perform could not have regular scenery : a few pieces of furniture would be brought or borrowed, with a throne suggesting a palace and a log of wood to signify part of the forest. The costumes would be limited by the money in hand, and there was little or no effort to be true to history. We have a picture of a performance of one of Shakespeare's plays set in ancient Rome, as it was acted in his time, and the clothes are a mixture of old Roman and new (i.e. Elizabethan) English. We may guess that the actors simply did their best with what they had, as we do when we play charades at home. They did, however, get some rich, fashionable garments of their own period in a roundabout way, since we are told that the noble-men used to give away their slightly used clothes to their servants and that these servants then sold them to the acting companies.

Such was the London and such the new industry of enter-tainment into which Will Shakespeare came. In many ways he was lucky. Marlowe had added to the public readiness to see plays, to hear resounding poetry, and to pay for their pleasures. Shakespeare could write as well as, and soon even better than, Marlowe. The theatre was growing in favour and finding more and more patrons. The great gentry were eager to help promising writers : it added to their glory if they had the best youngster of the day under their wing ; and Shakespeare was soon attached to one of the most famous of these lords. The making of music was now a regular habit in all homes, and new composers were increasing the fame of England as a musical country. The favourite instruments were the lute and the virginals (a kind of piano) and there was a new form of song, the madrigal, in which it was expected that all members of a household should be able to take a part. Shakespeare often mentioned in his plays the powers and charms of music ; so, as a music-lover moving in a world of madrigals and glees, this was very much the place, as well as the period, for him.

As a writer about men and their habits, their fashions and their follies, he could also draw richly upon the city life which he met at every turn. The long voyages of the sailors and explorers in the East and West Indies had opened up new knowledge and brought in new foods, rare spices, as well as the useful potato, and new pleasures, like smoking tobacco and sampling new wines.

The English travellers who went to Europe, and especially to France and Italy, came back with a load of new language as well as of new ideas. Shakespeare was to laugh at the dandies, whom he called water-flies after the gaily coloured dragonflies that flit over our streams in summer. He mocked their lisping use of strange foreign words ; but they were all good stuff for a man writing plays. The town was full not only of these chattering fops, but of cast-off soldiers and sailors, always ready to talk at large for the price of a meal or a drink. If their talk was not all true, then the writer could laugh at them as liars and boasters, which Shakespeare did. People sometimes wonder how Shakespeare came to know so much and so quickly about the world, and not his own England alone. The answer is that he had his eyes and his ears open, and that in the London of 1588, with the Spanish Armada defeated and with all the town lit up, he had plenty to see and hear, plenty to enjoy, and plenty stored up in his mind and waiting to be turned into stories and characters who have far outlived the age of their birth.

3

FOR the reasons which I have described, Shakespeare was determined to get on. He did get on, and that within a few years. Even if he had been tempted to be lazy, which he plainly was not, there were the pressures of his own poverty and of his need to send money home. He was entering a way of life which was growing continually wider and offering more and more chances to a clever and active young man. He had the existing actors and writers to watch, to rival, and to surpass. There was plenty of room for talent, and Shakespeare had brought with him to London a fine supply of words and thoughts and fancies to which his new life in the capital would add richly. When any clever youngster is full of these things he will readily pour them out, even if nobody wants them or will pay for them. But, in this case, with the growing appetite for plays and poetry, there was an expanding market for the seller.

About Shakespeare's first years in London we have no facts which can be called absolutely certain. We cannot expect a lot of information. Why should there be written records of what one obscure newcomer from the country was doing in a profession where there were many established and eminent people already at work? But, while we have no definite accounts of Shakespeare's rise, we do find remarks in the writings of the time which must almost certainly refer to him and signify that his emergence was being noted—and resented.

In 1592, when Shakespeare was twenty-eight, he had plainly made enough progress to annoy some of his seniors, An angry, disappointed, dying writer of plays, Robert Greene, described in his last book a person whom he called ' an upstart crow ' and a ' Johannes Factotum '. This creature, said Greene, thinks himself a fine poet, and ' the only Shake-scene in the country '. Together with this joke on Shakespeare's name and on his theatrical work went a jesting version of a line taken from a play already written (or partly written) by Shakespeare, a play about Henry VI and the Wars of the Roses. This sneer at a successful young man, made by an elder jealous of his success, indicates the position that Shakespeare had reached.

The words ' upstart crow ' mean that, in the opinion of Greene, here was no lark or nightingale among the poets, but only a harsh croaker. This only shows what a bad judge Greene, in his envy, could be. ' Johannes Factotum ' meant a jack of all trades. Greene was a writer and proud of his craft. Here, snarled he, is a pushing young fellow who is really only an actor ; yet he must butt into the writing business too. This was too much for Greene. He raged against the players who were now ' beautified with our feathers', i.e. dressed up with the quills of authors—and so putting

47

the ' rare wits ', as he called himself and his colleagues, out of work.

After Greene had died, the man who had issued his writings, Henry Chettle, made an apology for the rudeness and unfairness included in them. He did not mention Shakespeare by name, but he must have been referring to the ' upstart crow ' attacked by Greene, when he spoke of that maligned person as being both good-mannered and excellent at his work. Chettle added that ' divers of worship ' reported the young man's honesty and his skill in writing. ' Divers of worship ' means several people of high rank.

This lets us know that Shakespeare had done more than please his fellow-writers and employers. He had already been noticed by people of importance—courtiers, perhaps, and noblemen. To have ' friends at court ' was of great value in that period. London was still a small city and therefore offered only a small market for books and plays. So the money to be made, though useful, was not great unless there was some special success or some help from a kindly and wealthy admirer. The players, as we have seen, needed the protection of noblemen to keep them on the right side of the law : the poets needed the patronage of rich and eminent people who would thus call attention to their work, and who might also help them with money as well as with approval. Hence it was the habit of poets to dedicate their work to men of wealth and title who were already helping them or might do so in the future.

Shakespeare was lucky in finding such a champion. Just after Greene's attack on him, all the players in London suffered a disaster. The plague broke out in 1592 and raged for nearly two years. All the theatres were closed to prevent the spread

of infection. The actors could go on tour, which might not be rewarding, since visitors from the plague-stricken capital might well be unwelcome. The writers, however, could fill up the time by getting new plays ready for the reopening of the play-houses when the pestilence had passed. They could also write poetry for sale in book form. Shakespeare did both. He may have gone back to Stratford to do this work and so renewed his family life. But, as no actor's pay would be coming in, he would need the generosity of a patron to keep him going.

He certainly had a patron in the Earl of Southampton, and there was a later story told that this lord gave him a large sum of money. At any rate in 1593 and 1594 Shakespeare published two long poems called *Venus and Adonis* and *Lucrece*. Their titles show that they had classical subjects and they were written in a rather rich style that was then the fashion. They were both very popular, especially the first, and they had to be reprinted. Both were dedicated to the Earl of Southampton, and the second dedication suggested more warmth and intimacy than the first, as though the two men were now on friendly terms and were no longer lofty patron and humble favourite.

To have the freedom of a great lord's house and meet his company of friends would be a great privilege. Some people say that Shakespeare's plays cannot have been written by a man from a small country-town because they show so much knowledge of the grand way of life and of courtly manners and luxuries. At the Earl of Southampton's house Shakespeare could have met (or at least observed) the great political, legal and military figures of the day as well as the wits and musicians. I include the word ' legal ' because Southampton was a member of Gray's Inn, and the young men studying law who kept their terms there were much given to play-acting. It is known that Shakespeare's *Comedy of Errors* was performed in that Inn.

Southampton was nine years younger than Shakespeare and he may have been the handsome bachelor to whom Shakespeare wrote many of his sonnets, some of them advising marriage. But why and to whom the sonnets were written has remained an unsettled problem. What we do know is that there must have been a cordial relation between the two, and that this would enable the writer to meet or to watch such men of action as the fiery young Earl of Essex, Master of the Horse and also a commander against the Spanish at sea. Essex was one of Southampton's especial friends and is mentioned as a conqueror of rebellion in Ireland in Shakespeare's play of *Henry V*.

It has been suggested that Shakespeare spent the plague period, in part at least, in Southampton's country house, Titchfield, in Hampshire. It has also been suggested that either then or at some other time, Shakespeare went to Italy with Southampton : many of the plays have plots taken from Italian stories and consequently have Italian settings. Shakespeare seems to have known some geographical details about Italian cities, which caused the idea that he had actually been to these places instead of just reading about them. But we can only guess as to how the years were occupied when the London theatres were closed.

How many plays had Shakespeare written by the time the theatres reopened in 1594 ? Probably he had produced three plays about Henry VI and the Wars of the Roses. (Or at least he had had a large hand in these ; for two or three men to share the writing of a play was common practice then.) There was a Roman tragedy called *Titus Andronicus*, very crude and very popular. There were probably also two elementary comedies, *The Comedy of Errors* and *The Two Gentlemen of Verona*. Best of all was *Richard III*, a wonderful and richly dramatic picture of a king who was regarded as a complete scoundrel, but is now thought by many to have been not so bad and much wronged by his enemies' accounts of him. This piece would encourage Shakespeare's supporters to say that Marlowe had met his match. In our own time *Richard III* was made into a

superb film by Sir Laurence Olivier, who enlisted many of our leading actors to assist him.

At Christmas, 1594, we meet, in the records of the Lord Chamberlain, a clear and useful statement. Shakespeare is mentioned, along with Kemp, the comic actor, and Burbage, who was becoming the ' star ' actor of his age in serious parts, as providing two Court performances for Queen Elizabeth at Greenwich Palace. This means that by the time he was thirty Shakespeare was one of the three leaders of his company. We do not know in what companies he had served as a beginner. He may have had a place in the Earl of Derby's troupe, and there has been an attempt to show that he spent some of his youthful years as an apprentice player or musician in Lancashire, near that Earl's great house of Knowsley.

However this may be, the Derby team became, on the Earl's death, the Lord Chamberlain's Men, and it is as leaders of these that Shakespeare, Kemp and Burbage drew the money due to them for providing these ' command performances ' at Greenwich. On the death of Queen Elizabeth in 1603, King James, who succeeded her, took over the Chamberlain's Men and gave them a further royal patronage under the name of the King's Men. It was with this one company that Shakespeare worked for the rest of his life, both as actor and as writer. Other authors served several teams of players, as the chance arose. Shakespeare never left his early friends and colleagues, and they, of course, held on to him : for his fame was to rise rapidly in the years ahead, and a play by him was usually a great attraction.

His position had been strengthened by the death of the other play-maker most likely to draw money. The brilliant Christopher Marlowe was killed at the age of twenty-nine in 1593. This happened at a riverside inn after a dispute about the bill. Shakespeare was called ' gentle ' by those who knew him, but he lived in rough times when men carried swords and daggers and drew them too : tempers were fierce and duelling frequent. The disappearance of Marlowe, who wrote for a company called the Admiral's Men, made things easier for the rivals of that team. Shakespeare later expressed his mourning grief for Marlowe. But he profited by that tavern brawl.

There were great years ahead. Shakespeare seemed never to tire of writing, and he managed to keep on acting as well. There is not much known about his skill as a player, but it is certain that he went on performing as an actor long after he was a famous writer and very busy with his pen. It was said of him in later times that he had only small parts and that these were elderly characters. Two mentioned were the veteran servant, Adam, in *As You Like It* and the ghost of the murdered king in *Hamlet*. There is no report of his being a leading actor : indeed, he could hardly have found time to be that.

If Shakespeare had only small parts which meant short appearances on the stage, he would have had time during the rehearsals to direct the acting of the others. Nowadays, when we put on a play, there is a person in charge called the producer or director. His business is to arrange the moves, regulate the speech, and improve the methods of the players. We do not know how long the companies in Shakespeare's time rehearsed a play or who controlled the rehearsals. As each company had quite a number of plays in hand at the same time and could switch from one to another according to the public demand, it seems likely that the rehearsals would be fewer and simpler than are usual in our theatres now. The best Shakespearian performances of today, those which you might see in London or at Stratford-upon-Avon, have probably had at least a month or even more of very careful preparation. I think that Shakespeare's fellows would have been greatly surprised at this. Of course, if they played in the open theatres, which I have described, there was no lighting to arrange and almost no scenery to plan or move ; but they had to have furniture, weapons, costumes, and other ' properties ', as we call them, made ready. The business of mounting a play was plainly carried out in a thrifty way.

I have already mentioned their ways of dressing the actors, and the actors themselves were not many in number. All except those who took the chief roles had to ' double ' or ' treble ' other parts ; that is to say, that they had to keep coming on as a second or third character after their first appearance. A Swiss traveller who saw a performance of

Julius Caesar in 1599 says that it was done with fifteen players :
if you count the list of persons appearing in the play, apart
from members of the crowd, there are as many as thirty-five.
In a modern theatre you may see quite a number of players
appearing in the crowd-scenes and battle-scenes which Shakespeare's plays demand.   But Shakespeare himself complained
about and apologised for his scanty company.   Few plays
demand more show of armies in the field than does *Henry V* ;
in that case Shakespeare arranged for a Speaker, called the
Chorus, to explain, between the various parts or ' acts ', as
we now call them, how much the audience must use its own
fancy to imagine the fleets and armies and the warlike scenes.

The Chorus says that he is sorry that they have to present the great battle of Agincourt ' with four or five most vile and ragged foils '—which means with only four or five swordsmen who did not know much about fighting ! So if Shakespeare, being a minor actor as well as a major author, had to organise the staging of his plays and arrange the crowd and battle-scenes, he certainly had his work cut out.

With the plague over and the theatres busy and successful, Shakespeare's great years began. He wrote one fine tragedy, that of the young, ill-fated lovers *Romeo and Juliet*, but mostly he was busy for the next six years with comedies and historical dramas. Within four years he had added eight more to the plays that I have already mentioned. These included such favourite comedies as *A Midsummer Night's Dream*, *The Merchant of Venice*, and the histories of *Richard II*, *Henry IV* (in two parts) and *King John*.

In 1596 there was a tragedy in his own life. His only son, Hamnet, died in August of that year at the age of eleven. Shakespeare himself may have hurried back to Stratford in order to be beside the boy in his illness. It happens that he was writing the play of *King John* just about that time and this play includes some very moving lines about the death of the young Prince Arthur. He is described as looking

hollow as a ghost,

As dim and meagre as an ague's fit.

58

The mourning mother cries :

> *Grief fills the room up of my absent child,*
> *Lies in his bed, walks up and down with me,*
> *Puts on his pretty looks, repeats his words,*

and she ends with lamenting the loss of

> *my fair son,*
> *My life, my joy, my food, my all the world.*

If this play was indeed being written at the time of Hamnet's fatal illness, it is natural to believe that Shakespeare was pouring into these lines his own grief for the boy who had wasted away, so dim and meagre, and whose memory was thus haunting, with looks and words, his bereaved parents.

But all was not sadness at Stratford. In the following summer Shakespeare was able to buy the finest home in the town, New Place, which had been described before then as a ' pretty house of brick and timber '—that is to say, with the cross-beams which you can see in so many houses of the period. It cost sixty pounds, which sounds little to us, but was a big sum in those times. This meant not only that Shakespeare had become prosperous, but that he could prove to his own family and to all their neighbours in the town that the youngster who had joined the vagabond players so boldly and gone to seek his fortune in London, had, as we say, ' made good '. He was already a man of some wealth and, what was more, he had enough influence in London to provide

that his father's petition for a grant of arms with a motto was admitted.

Both old John and young Will Shakespeare were now to have the word Gentleman written after their names. Their motto was *Non Sans Droict*, French for 'Not Without Right'. The coat of arms had on it a spear and a falcon. Unfortunately New Place was stupidly pulled down by its owner a century and a half later. Now there is a Museum on the spot and an exquisitely kept garden in which are planted all the flowers that are mentioned in Shakespeare's plays. Will Shakespeare's entry into the town's Big House was followed by further purchase of land in Stratford. So it was plain to all that the son, suspected by some of taking up an unworthy career, had brought prosperity and honour to his family within ten years of his leaving home.

Back in London, Shakespeare was soon to create one of his most famous characters, that of the fat knight Sir John Falstaff who appears in the two history-plays of *Henry IV* and also in the comedy of *The Merry Wives of Windsor* Falstaff's death is recorded in the play of *Henry V*. Sir John, a ludicrous figure with his tremendous bulk, his bragging of his valour, but with his cowardly performances, at once became a great favourite of the public. A young admirer of Shakespeare in his own time wrote verses in his hero's memory and said that, whenever Falstaff was to be on the stage,

> *You scarce shall have a room,*
> *All is so pestered.*

This meant, of course, that there was a great rush for seats and that one would be lucky to get in at all. Sir John has been the joy of play-goers ever since. One of the greatest actors of the part in our time has been Sir Ralph Richardson.

Back in London, Shakespeare found constant demands for his writing, and he met those demands with a plentiful output of plays. Between 1596 and 1600 or 1601 he added to his list a play on an ancient Roman subject, *Julius Caesar*, as well as completing his English history-plays. It was at this time that he came to the height of his skill in composing comedies with most fascinating heroines. Three plays of this kind, *Much Ado About Nothing*, *As You Like It* and *Twelfth Night* were written about the turn of the century, and it seems that Shakespeare's company must then have contained a very clever boy-actor who could learn such long and important parts as those of the young women who dominate these plays, Beatrice, Rosalind and Viola.

If the dramatist could not rely on these roles being skilfully performed by a lad who could bring out the art of the prose and the beauty of the poetry, he surely would not have written them. We must always remember that Shakespeare was not an author who sat remote and worked in isolation ; he was one of a team, serving their interests and listening to their demands, and often acting as well as writing. We know that in 1598, when he was most active with his pen, he was one of the cast in a play called *Every Man in his Humour* written by Ben Jonson, a man who was to rise to a great position in the theatre and to be made Poet Laureate.

During this period Shakespeare was living in Southwark, near the theatres on the South Bank of the Thames. It was then that, in the winter of 1598-9, he and his fellows were able to build a new theatre which they called the Globe. It was to become, chiefly because of Shakespeare, the most famous of the London theatres. It came to be set up in a very curious way. He and his colleagues Cuthbert and Richard Burbage were losing the lease of their play-house in North London called The Theatre : the owner of the site wanted to be rid of the place. But the structure belonged to the players, and so, taking the law into their own hands (and saws and axes too), they simply pulled down and removed the woodwork. This gave them the material for a new start : obtaining a lease on the South Bank, they had a new play-house quickly built in a position of more value and convenience than any in North London.

In this new venture Shakespeare had a tenth share, so that, if its plays were popular, he drew some of the profits as well as

his fees for writing and acting. One of his first contributions
to this new Globe Theatre was the tragedy of *Hamlet*, which
many think his greatest play. Certainly it was very much
discussed ; it was read in printed editions and acted at the
universities as well as by the professional players. A few years
later we even hear of its being performed by sailors at sea.
There was an odd reason given for this : the captain of the
ship thought that performing plays kept his men from ' idleness,
sleep, and unlawful games '.

In 1601 there were exciting events in London and these involved Shakespeare's early and generous patron, the Earl of Southampton, and Shakespeare's own company too. The bold and restless Earl of Essex, having quarrelled with the Queen, actually attempted to lead a rebellion against her. Southampton was one of his comrades in this folly. Immediately before their mad rising the Lord Chamberlain's Men were engaged at a special fee to revive Shakespeare's tragedy of *Richard II* because this showed a king being turned off his throne. The message to the public would be that monarchs can be successfully deposed.

The revolt was a complete failure. Essex rushed back to

London from Ireland to plead with the Queen for his life. But by bursting into Elizabeth's dressing-room he only increased her anger. He was tried for treason and executed, and Southampton also was condemned to death; but his sentence was altered to imprisonment, and he went to the Tower of London. Shakespeare's company had to explain their part in the affair, and evidently they were able to plead ignorance of the reason why they were asked to stage *Richard II*. They were forgiven and actually gave a command performance at Whitehall—not, of course, of *Richard II*—on the eve of the execution of Essex.

This foolish outbreak, with its terrible results, must have

greatly distressed Shakespeare, as he had been so closely linked with Southampton who had risked his life and was now to spend two years in gaol. King James VI of Scotland who, as James I of England, succeeded Queen Elizabeth after her death in March 1603, released the Earl at once ; he also showed particular favour to the players, honouring the Lord Chamberlain's Men with the new title of the King's Men. They were given special licence to use and exercise the ' art and faculty of playing ' far and wide. Shakespeare's name came second on the list of the company, being preceded only by that of Laurence Fletcher, a favourite comedian whom the King had brought with him from Scotland. The King's Men attended the Coronation and were given a special allowance of red cloth for uniforms on that occasion.

What meanwhile was happening at Stratford ? John Shakespeare, Will's father, died in the autumn of 1601 ; he had had his troubled times, but now he had happily reached a ripe age in comfort. He had seen his son prosper and the family honoured with the coat of arms that he had coveted. Shakespeare's mother died seven years after his father. Will, however much London claimed his labours, kept his eye on his home-town, and during the coming years was often adding to his property by buying land or cottages. He need not have been there to oversee these deals : his younger brother Gilbert certainly acted for him on one occasion and may have been his regular agent. Shakespeare had responded to the vitality and the variety of London life with alacrity ; but he never ceased to be in part a countryman, and the language in his plays continued to be full of words and phrases recalling the riverside and the water-meadows with their flowers, beasts and birds.

Between Shakespeare's home at New Place and the parish church at Stratford there had settled a medical doctor called John Hall. He had studied at Cambridge and in France and soon won a high reputation in the English Midlands for his skill in curing invalids. He was not just a humble local figure : lords and ladies summoned him from considerable distances. He was acclaimed ; he prospered ; he took a good house with a good garden which you may explore today. Shakespeare's New Place has vanished, but Hall's Croft, as the house is called, remains and can be visited.

Meanwhile Shakespeare's first child, Susanna, was reaching a marriageable age and the Doctor was a close neighbour as well as a good match. Her wedding with Dr Hall took place in the summer of 1607. As the epitaph on her grave in Stratford shows, she had a reputation for being wise and witty. So the children of such an able pair as Dr and Mistress Hall, with such a remarkable grandfather, should have been wonderful people. But there was no male heir and the one daughter, Elizabeth, lacked the chance of a career that a girl coming from such a family would have today. She was twice married, but had no children. Since Shakespeare's son Hamnet was already dead, and since the two sons of his second daughter Judith died young and without heirs, there were no direct descendants of the great man after the death in 1670 of Elizabeth, who had been first Mrs Nash and then Lady

Bernard. The Shakespeare line has only been continued through his sister Joan, who married a Stratford hat-maker called Hart.

There is a tradition that Dr Hall was a Puritan and therefore must have disapproved of his father-in-law's way of life in the theatre ; but, had there been any deep disapproval, the marriage with Susanna would have been unlikely.

It can be noticed that after the date of Dr Hall's arrival in Stratford there is more mention of illnesses in Shakespeare's plays, and sometimes a number of strange medical terms are listed. So it is possible, and even probable, that Shakespeare, who was so keen an observer of every phase of life, was deeply interested in his neighbour's practice and dispensary and enjoyed talking over the problems of health and disease. Dr Hall kept a record of his cases : he wrote in Latin and the book has been translated. Unfortunately he did not begin to make his notes until a year after his famous father-in-law had died.

In London the King's Men profited by the new monarch's liking for plays and masques. But the mood of the city became sombre. James was easily influenced by his favourites at Court, and the Court contained some very shifty characters. There was a natural regret that the great Queen Elizabeth had passed and that a reign so fortunate for England's standing among the nations was over. For some reason, Shakespeare suddenly began to leave laughter out of his plays : he was now engaged on the great tragedies in which a bleak world replaces the blithe one of the comedies. For some years there was to be no more display of fancy free and of sparkling wit.

We cannot say why this occurred. Some scholars suggest that the fashion for comedies was passing, and that there was a new taste for tragic themes : therefore Shakespeare, being, as the players often call themselves, a servant of the public, served up his plays of crime and punishment and of human frailty and folly coming to a sad end. Another view is that Shakespeare was hit by some illness which severely depressed his spirits, or by some suffering in his private life which made him see mainly the worst side of human nature and the cruelty of human destiny. Whatever the explanation may be, there is no doubt that this dark period of his writing produced plays of rare depth worked out in language, both in prose and poetry, which revealed the greatest force and beauty ever achieved in our tongue. After *Hamlet* came the study of vicious jealousy in *Othello*, vicious ambition in *Macbeth*, and of vicious vanity and selfish folly in *King Lear*. Other tragedies followed, including one about the Roman general Antony and the Egyptian queen Cleopatra which can be placed with the other masterpieces as sharing the summit of all Shakespeare's labours.

4

THE year of 1608 was an important one in Shakespeare's life. It began with a sad personal loss. His youngest brother, Edmund, sixteen years his junior, died at the turn of the year : he had followed Will's steps to London and had become an actor : what company he served we do not know, but evidently he had some position, since his burial was in the great church of St Mary's on the Bankside, the building that is now South-wark Cathedral. It was marked by ' a fore-noon knell of the great bell '. That was a farewell salutation unlikely to have been granted to a man of no position, but the elder brother's interest may have helped to obtain this honour for Edmund.

After the personal loss came a personal gain. Two months later there was born in Stratford his granddaughter, Elizabeth Hall. In the late summer there was a professional change in the mounting fortunes of the King's Men. They now added to their tenancy of the Globe Theatre on the Bankside the occupation of the Blackfriars Theatre on the north side of the river. This had for some time been successfully worked by one of the juvenile companies, known as the Children of the Chapel. They must have been losing their long-held popularity, since the managers in 1608, Evans and Giles, were ready to give up their lease. The King's Men then used the theatre themselves and Shakespeare had a share of one-seventh in the venture. We know that some of the boys, now growing up, were taken over as adult actors by the new management.

The Blackfriars was a roofed-in theatre and thus had to be artificially lit. It could give evening performances which the open, day-lit Globe did not. The Blackfriars, being more comfortable, had a different and more fashionable audience. Its stage offered much better opportunity for scenic effect, and in the plays that Shakespeare wrote after 1608 there is allowance made for these conditions.

He introduced masques, which we might call tableaux or picture-scenes : in a romantic setting gods and goddesses might appear being lowered from the roof. There was a growing taste for spectacle of this kind, and Shakespeare, though he may not have liked this taste, was ready to serve it.

72

The fashion in play-making now began to alter considerably. After 1608 Shakespeare abandoned tragedy. Either he felt that he had worked out his dark view of life or else he was giving way to the demands of the new public for a light, fantastical, and decorative kind of play. He may also have been yielding to the pressure of his company who wanted to keep up with prevailing fashions. At any rate he now composed romantic pieces with a fairy-tale kind of plot and scope for these curious masques which needed elaborate stage-craft and some machinery. In a queer play about early Britain, called *Cymbeline*, there

is a masque which introduces, with suitable music, several ghosts. Here is one of the stage directions : ' Jupiter descends in thunder and lightning, sitting upon an eagle : he throws a thunder-bolt : the ghosts fall on their knees.'

That obviously involves careful and costly production : the actor who played Jupiter would insist that his seat upon the descending eagle was a safe one, and the players of the ghosts would also insist that the thunderbolt did not create too powerful an explosion. So the rehearsing of these later, more fantastic pieces, *Cymbeline*, *A Winter's Tale* and *The Tempest*, probably given in 1609, 1610 and 1611, must have been much more careful than was the preparation of the previous plays. Those, far stronger in drama, had been far simpler in their call upon the company's resources. *The Tempest* called not only for a masque of reapers and nymphs, who finally vanish amid ' a strange, hollow and confused noise ', but also for magical effects such as the disappearance of a banquet that had been laid. It is made plain by the exacting stage direc-tions that in the new kind of theatre a new kind of stage-craft was being introduced. The result was in many ways much more like the productions to which we are accustomed today in spectacular shows and pantomimes.

This had its dangers. In 1613 the Globe Theatre was burned down during the performance of Shakespeare's last play, a historical piece about Henry VIII, of which a col-league, John Fletcher, may have been part author. This play included big processions in the popular style of masque and also a ceremonial firing of cannon. Since the Globe Theatre had a thatched roof over the closed-in part, there was risk of fire ; the disaster occurred when some of the inflammable stuff discharged from the cannon was left smouldering in the roof. The audience was so much engrossed by the play, reported a spectator, that at first too little notice was taken of the accident. Owing to this carelessness the whole building caught fire and was destroyed. Luckily both players and spectators got away in time. ' Only one man had his breeches set on fire, that would perhaps have broiled him, if he had not by the benefit of a provident wit put it out with bottle ale.' It was indeed fortunate that refreshments were served ! The Globe was immediately rebuilt with a tiled roof in place of the dangerous thatch, and was reopened in June of 1614. The loss to the company, who had to pay fourteen hundred pounds for the new theatre, was a heavy one, and Shakespeare would have suffered with the rest.

In the year 1608, or a little after, Shakespeare seems to have retired to a great extent from his London life and to be spending far more of his time at home in Stratford. He could write his last plays in the peace of the countryside, and they do contain some evidence of his growing affection for pastoral events and the flowers of an English garden. His mother died in 1609, but he had with him his wife, now an ageing woman, his two daughters, Susanna Hall and Judith who married a

75

neighbour, Thomas Quiney, just before her father's death, and his grandchild, Elizabeth Hall. He revealed, in these last pieces, a devotion to young girlish heroines, women of innocence. It is true that some of the old bitterness occasionally broke in, and that he could still depict ugly passions with tremendous force. But there is, over and around these plays, a calmness and a happiness which had been absent from his work of the previous ten years when he was writing the great tragedies about broken lives and a world of ruthless people.

Will Shakespeare was once more at home, watching his little family group develop and his property grow larger with new purchases. He was only about forty-five years old when he began to write these last plays. To us that seems just the entry to middle-age, but to people of his period it was the beginning of decline. He himself talked of forty winters besieging his brow as though forty was the time of wrinkled old age. He had been working at a tremendous pace as he combined his acting with writing plays, looking after rehearsals, and sharing the cares of management. There had been profits : he was now a man of some wealth in the eyes of Stratford : he had much to be proud of ; but also there had been much to tire him out.

Reports had come to London of English mariners wrecked in western seas. So in 1611 he wrote his famous and fanciful play of a far-off coral island. It was called *The Tempest* because in it a great storm destroys a ship and throws its company on the yellow sands. Here they meet Prospero, a wise and lordly man of magic, now in exile and living with his daughter in a cave. At the end of the play Prospero determines to abandon his magical arts, and it is generally believed that Shakespeare was thinking of his own resolve and making Prospero his spokesman. In his two speeches of farewell to wizardry, Prospero uses words that indicate a personal meaning. He talks of his actors, his revels, and 'the great globe itself', which may well refer to the King's Men and their play-house. Also he complains of fatigue and brain-storms. By retiring into his cell (perhaps a symbol for the quiet country) he will seek to heal his 'infirmity' and cool his 'beating mind' and 'troubled brain'. We cannot be sure that Shakespeare was writing of himself and of some weakness that had come upon him, but it is likely enough.

He did, in fact, set to work again on the play already mentioned, *Henry VIII*. A new writer, John Fletcher, had arrived to compose popular pieces for the King's Men, and it is possible that he began this piece about Henry VIII and the birth of Queen Elizabeth, and that it seemed to the actors not good enough. They may have asked Shakespeare to break into his leisure and rewrite the play. Then he may have agreed to do so, since he was not at all proud and, even at the top of his success, he had shown that he was ready to patch up the work of much lesser men for the benefit of his company.

Whatever the truth about *Henry VIII*, we can take *The*

79

Tempest to be the last outpouring of his finest poetry. It was well liked and was chosen to be one of the plays performed in the royal revels which followed the wedding of King James's daughter Elizabeth to a Germanic prince. It was through this marriage, incidentally, that our present royal family came to inherit the crown which the House of Stuart lost and could not regain.

In the brief epilogue (last words) of *The Tempest*, which is appointed to be spoken by Prospero himself, there is the appeal, usual in epilogues, for applause. There is also this statement of his purpose, which was surely Shakespeare's too,

> *Gentle breath of yours my sails*
> *Must fill, or else my project fails,*
> *Which was to please : now I want*
> *Spirits to enforce, art to enchant.*

In other words, Shakespeare had lived to delight the public, and now he felt that his power to cast the old spell upon an audience was failing him. So he asked, in words, for their mercy and their prayers.

There is much pathos in those lines. But their author was not finished yet. He lived on for five years after he wrote *The Tempest*, and for four years after he did his share in *Henry VIII*. We know that his house in Stratford provided entertainment to strangers. We know that he was alive, though perhaps an invalid, when his second daughter, Judith, was married in

February 1616. Two months later, on his birthday, 23 April, he was dead. He was then exactly fifty-two years old.

He had signed the final version of his will a month before

that. It has been preserved and is at Somerset House, among myriads of other wills, in London. The bulk of his property went to Susanna Hall. His widow was protected by what was called the ' right of dower ' which insured her a home at New Place, and a third of his rents from holdings of land. She was also given his ' second-best bed ' : the best bed may have been in the guest-room. Judith received a marriage-portion ; his sister, Mrs Hart, had her share, and there were gifts to neighbours in Stratford. Three of his fellow players in London were left money to buy rings in memory of their dead friend. Two of them called Heminge and Condell collected, edited and published his plays in a single large volume known as the First Folio. This appeared in 1623, the year in which Anne, his widow, died at the age of sixty-seven.

Half his plays had been printed singly in smaller books called Quartos, mostly in the middle of his career. In those times the text of a play belonged to the company for which it was written, but sometimes it might be stolen by rivals ; or it might be published for sale if the money to be made was badly needed. The more successful did Shakespeare's plays become, the more carefully did the King's Men hold on to the texts, because they did not want other actors to get hold of them and use them. If Heminge and Condell had died early or been neglectful, and so had not carried out the great work of collecting all thirty-six plays by Shakespeare and issuing them in the First Folio, the world would have had only eighteen, and some of those in crude and shortened form. So we owe to these two men the saving of the finest plays in our language.

In the Folio volume there were included verses written by friends and admirers. One set of these was by Shakespeare's rival, Ben Jonson. It included, among much eloquent tribute, the famous line

He was not of an age, but for all time.

Ben Jonson's forecast has come true. The work of Shakespeare has been studied, read and acted as the work of no other man of the theatre ; it has been discussed and argued about as that of no other author. The books about him are innumerable and sometimes over-learned. Shakespeare has sometimes been made to seem dull, no better than a school-room subject. That is wrong. He put life and laughter before learning. We must never forget those last lines spoken by Prospero and, seemingly, by Shakespeare himself. His purpose was 'to please'. He had given, and continually gives, immense pleasure and in his life he had been pleasant too.

We do not know what caused his death ; the story of a too merry meeting with some of his London friends and a fatal carouse is probably a fiction. From his signatures it seems that he was very weak before he died. One does not see him at any time as a tough Elizabethan type who could batter his way through life without exhaustion. 'Our little life is rounded with a sleep,' said Prospero. And now the tired man slept.

All that was said of him in his time, except in jealousy, repeated the praise of his gentleness—that is to say, his good manners and friendliness. He was not of the quarrelsome, duelling kind. Yet we must not think, because of this stress on ' gentle Mr Shakespeare ' and his civil ways, that he was lacking in character. He flashed wit : he made game of those who posed and were pretentious. He liked to make money and to invest it carefully. He loved beauty in all its forms and told that love in several ways. Sometimes he used small words very simply and sometimes big words very richly. He could speak for mankind in all its moods and find always the perfect word and phrase for what we feel and are and seem. His life was not long in years, but the memory of it will always endure.